HERE, I CAN BREATHE

An anthology of
poems inspired by the
natural world and life
in the countryside

BY

CHRYSSA TURNER

First published in the United Kingdom in 2024 by
The Choir Press

ISBN 978-1-78963-513-3

For Mum and Dad,
with all my love

PREFACE

Growing up in rural South Devon, with cows grazing over my garden fence and a view of Dartmoor across the neighbouring fields, my love of the countryside stems from a very young age. Childhood walking holidays with my parents and brother furthered my enjoyment of being out in the open air, and instilled a love of hiking which is still enjoyed today.

Nature inspires much of my poetry. In this collection, inspiration came from walks at both ends of England, including along the South West Coast Path and amongst the Lake District fells, and from holidays abroad to other parts of Europe. Some are narrative poems, others more generally describe the countryside observed, or the feelings engendered, whilst being in the open air. I have included my own version of the Countryside Code, as well as poems about that good old British favourite, the weather!

Poems often start to form in my head as I walk. As a result, I now always carry a notebook and pen in my rucksack. I well remember stopping near the beginning of a walk along the coast path in North Devon, to write down the opening lines of *Clovelly, Westwards*, before I forgot them. I also make good use of the record function on my phone, especially on my daily dog-walks.

Nature is not all sunshine and roses, though, and some poems deal with less welcome aspects, most notably of the weather. 'Wild' weather is no less awe-inspiring than brilliant sunshine, but perhaps not always quite so enjoyable (although that is, of course, a matter of personal preference).

Whatever your own experiences of nature and of the countryside, I hope that reading these poems brings you much enjoyment.

CT

CONTENTS

PARTICULAR PLACES

A COUNTRY CALENDAR

APERITIF

WORD PAINTING

If a picture paints a thousand words,
Can the opposite be true?
The phrases I craft lovingly,
A gift, from me to you.

To paint a picture in your mind,
Or stir a memory,
Each word chosen carefully,
An image to portray.

So read my verses thoughtfully,
Consider them with care,
Let the words play in your mind,
And turn and tumble there.

I pray the images I paint
In your own mind you'll see,
By dint of careful poetry,
A gift to you, from me.

MORNING

DAWN

In the quiet calm of pre-dawn,
Morning waits, perfectly poised,
Like a gently coiled spring,
Ready for slow-action release.

At a preordained signal,
The spring is sprung;
Little by little,
With clockwork precision,
Like a slowly opening flower,
A brand-new day unfolds.

DAWN CHORUS

As night wears on and day draws nigh,
A hint of light creeps across the sky.

Sound erupts – no bird is dumb!
So glad are they that dawn has come.

They sing out lustily to greet the day,
Each in his own peculiar way.

Peace returns as the sky grows light,
Marking the end of a long dark night.

UNRIVALLED MORNING FRESHNESS

Unrivalled morning freshness!
Be it summer sun, autumn mist or winter
    chill,
Nature yawns and kicks off the
    bedclothes,
While much of humanity slumbers still.

The slate wiped clean by dark and
    dreaming,
Each new dawn brings fresh promises,
Renewed hope, new opportunities;
Unending possibilities beckon.

Soon, day-to-day normality resuming,
Mundane bustle will engulf us,
But here, in the unrivalled morning
    freshness,
Caught between sleep and duty,
All is calm,
The world awaits.

AN ALMOST-PERFECT MORNING

I pull the cottage door to, behind me,
And step out into the cool, crisp morning;
Whistling to you in my memory,
I see you trotting alongside me -
Tail high, ears alert, nose sniffing
The multitudinous scents of a brand-new
    day.

Little traffic traverses the dead-end lane,
So you run unencumbered by leash,
Free to follow the tantalising cacophony
Of scents, that only you can smell.
Whose nocturnal trail are you following?
Who has already stepped this way, today?

Passing the last few sleepy cottages,
We head on down the dewy field,
You zig-zag your way, attention caught
By one trail after another.
The mustiness of the ever-smouldering
    bonfire
Assaults my nostrils,
But many more clamour for your
    attention,
And, happily, you follow them all;
You are the epitome of bliss.

I breathe deeply, inhaling the freshness
Of a yet-unsullied morning,
The sun, breaking through an early mist,
Promises a perfect day...
If only you were running with me still.

SUNLIT MORNING

Sun slants horizontally across the
    tranquil meadow,
Lighting up the morning with a fiery
    glow,
Overnight cobwebs, heavy with dew,
Sparkle in the hedges like a thousand tiny
    diamonds.

The air is still, the brook barely ripples,
Motes of dust dance idly in the golden
    rays,
As every bird sings with unbridled joy,
This beautiful sunlit morning.

EASTER MORNING

The heady scent of daffodils assaults my
    nostrils,
As I gently push open the heavy wooden
    door;
The tiny village church, overflowing with
    spring flowers,
Welcomes and embraces me, on Easter
    morning.

Vases perch haphazardly on every ledge
    and window-sill,
Daffodils garnered from every village
    garden,
Posies full of primroses cram along the
    pulpit edge,
Bursting forth with joy on Easter
    morning.

After the eternity of cold, barren Lent,
Bright yellows, like a thousand suns,
    shine brightly all around me,
Their fresh fragrance filling the cool
    spring air,
Mirroring the miracle of Easter morning.

Like an aromatic photograph lodged deep
   within my memory,
I cannot smell a daffodil but I am there
   again,
In that tiny village church, more than
   half a lifetime later,
Reliving the joy of my childhood Easter
   morning.

FLORA AND FAUNA

HERE, I CAN BREATHE

Where early morning dew glistens like
    diamonds,
And lacy-leaved trees are bejewelled by
    sunlight,
Where azaleas in every hue from white
    through to purple
Ignite the banks, the hedgerows and
    gardens,
Their colours complementing the bright
    spring green,
The perfect stage-set to the background
    fells,
Where an orchestra of never-tiring birds
Creates a soothing balm of perpetual
    music,
And fresh mountain air inflates my weary
    lungs,
Here, where the birds serenade me,
Here, where the cuckoo calls me,
Here, where nature caresses me,
Here, I can breathe.

ANCIENT TREES

Caught by golden rays of the low-slung
   sun,
Midges dance crazily over the water,
Adjacent a tunnel of ancient trees.

In old tractor ruts, thick mud lingers,
Squidgy and squelchy and deep,
In the cool dark shade of the ancient
   trees.

When the sun dons a cloak of darkest
   cloud,
And the rains pour suddenly down,
Walkers shelter beneath the ancient
   trees.

Cool in heatwaves, refuge in rainstorms,
A peaceful spot to meander and dream,
Beside the brook, under the ancient
   trees.

BLACKBERRYING *(a haiku)*

Blackberrying time!
We must go and harvest them -
Wastage is a crime.

BLUEBELLS

Splashes of blue in bright, spring-green
   hedges,
In shady woods, around field edges,
If every flower held a single bell,
On windy days, how the sound would
   swell!
Would rise and fall with every breeze,
Along the lanes, amongst the trees,
Ringing out, in vales and dells,
Fairy music from tiny bells.

BLUEBELL WOODS

A carpet of bluebells stretches out,
As far as the eye can see,
Shimmering lilac, lit by the sun
That filters in through the trees.

A snapshot of memory enters my head,
Of carefree childhood days,
Playing in magical woods like these,
Warmed by the sun's bright rays.

BUTTERCUPS

Buttercup meadows create a golden glow,
Particularly welcome on dull, grey days;
Like the flowering fields of oilseed rape,
They reflect the sunshine that isn't there.

DAFFODILS

Golden daffodils,
Faces uplifted to the gentle sun,
Basking in the welcome of her warming
   rays,
Harbingers of spring and the lengthening
   of days.

Rain-drenched daffodils,
Heads bowed down under the weight of
   water,
Patiently awaiting the return of
   sunshine,
Enduring the wind-blown seasonal
   storms.

Snow-covered daffodils,
Blooms encrusted in icy jackets,
Splashes of yellow peeking through a
   white blanket,
Withstanding unfriendly winter weather.

Golden daffodils,
Harbingers of spring
And the lengthening of days.

FOXGLOVES

Purple foxgloves, stately, tall,
Peering over hedge and wall,
Imperiously watching
The minutiae of life.

Tiny bell-shaped flowers,
Entrance insects for hours,
Their stately beauty hiding
A deadly secret truth.

FORGET-ME-NOTS

Blue and pink forget-me-nots
with bright golden centres,
delicately decorate
spring lanes and gardens.

Each individual flower-head,
a tiny pentamerous miracle,
as if painted by the finest brush,
delicately held in a master's hand.

A gift said to symbolise true love,
their miniature perfection,
like a finely-crafted ornament,
beautiful to behold.

HORSE CHESTNUT TREES

Horse chestnut leaves are turning brown
As I wander by the brook,
Though leafy green so recently,
Soon will wear their winter look.

The conkers, thick upon the ground,
An age-old, new-found joy,
Would once be laced upon a string,
And be a treasured toy.

Now banned from many playgrounds,
They lie upon the ground,
And make a shiny, cobbled path,
Waiting to be found.

Along the path, like rowing boats
Washed up upon the tide,
Beside the rich brown conkers, lie
Their shells, split open wide.

From bright green leaves and 'candles'
In their glorious springtime best,
Through a harbinger of autumn,
To a well-earned winter rest.

LIRIODENDRON CHINENSE

Sitting in the shade of a Chinese Tulip
    Tree,
September sunshine streaming through
    its leaves,
The wind whispers softly, cooling my
    coffee,
And all around me is peace - perfect
    peace.

A rural scene spreads out before me,
Of golden fields and hazy hills,
Late summer laziness bewitches the
    garden,
Where all the world is calm and still.

Sitting in the shade, leaves swaying
    gently,
Enjoying the head gardener's legacy,
The world is manic, but not where I'm
    sitting,
In the shade of his Chinese Tulip Tree.

SUMMER FLOWERS

Pink and white foxgloves, stately and
    tall,
Honeysuckle climbing on hedgerow and
    wall,
Campion, pink, with red and white clover,
Appear on the roadsides, over and over.

Forget-me-not, speedwell and cornflower,
    blue,
Provide cool colours for the rainbow hue,
Plump purple thistles like miniature
    crowns,
Tall meadow grasses in yellows and
    browns.

Wild roses rambling by gate and o'er
    hedge,
Scarlet red poppies around field-edge,
Corn and marsh marigolds, dandelions,
    too,
Add yellow splashes to both red and blue.

A positive paintbox of colours on show,
As nature lights up with a rich golden
   glow,
In fields and woodlands, on roadsides and
   banks,
For the wild flowers of summer, we give
   heartfelt thanks!

SNOWDROPS

Tiny pearls of promise,
Poking up their heads
When winter chills abound,
Nature's assurance that
Spring will come.

The first signs of hope,
Post-Christmas,
In a cold and frozen world.

FEATHERED FRENZY

Robin alights on my garden spade,
eager for easy worms.
Shy sparrows observe us
from vantage spot close by,
courage failing in human company.

Nearby, an invisible woodpecker
goes about his noisy business,
heralding spring.
Clumsy pigeons crash-land
on swaying branches overhead,
whilst delicate blue-tits
flit about the garden,
with scarce an arboreal movement.

Families of finches
feast hungrily on proffered seeds,
darting to and from the table,
relishing a ready meal,
scattering crumbs
for ground-feeders to scavenge.

A lone blackbird sings his heart out
from a lofty bough,
cheering me in my endeavours.
Half-hidden but so clearly heard,
his sweet song makes my spirits soar.

All around the garden, a feathered frenzy,
each following his own particular path.
Here, as everywhere, nature moves
to her own special rhythms,
but despite such frantic activity,
all is calm in my peaceful garden.

MOLE INVASION *(a haiku)*

Soft brown mounds of earth,
Haphazard across my lawn -
The moles have returned!

HERDWICK SHEEP

Black, white, brown and all shades of
   grey,
On roadside verges, fields and fellsides,
Inquisitive faces behind drystone walls.

Grey as the Lakeland slate around you,
Black as the thunder-clouds threatening
   rain,
White as the snow that hides you in
   Winter.

Symbolic of the Lakeland fells,
As timeless as the rugged landscape,
Blending with your rocky fellsides.

Grey as the Lakeland slate around you,
Black as the thunder-clouds threatening
   rain,
White as the snow that hides you in
   Winter.

Ancient multi-purpose breed,
Hardy natives, your thick woollen coats
The perfect foil for persistent Lakeland
   rain.

Grey as the Lakeland slate around you,
Black as the thunder-clouds threatening
    rain,
White as the snow that hides you in
    Winter.

Regular escapologists,
Frequently found the wrong side of a
    fence,
Wandering along the steep mountain
    roads.

Grey as the Lakeland slate around you,
Black as the thunder-clouds threatening
    rain,
White as the snow that hides you in
    Winter.

Black, white, brown and all shades of
    grey,
On roadside verges, fields and fellsides,
Inquisitive faces of Herdwick sheep.

RIVERS AND SEAS

DEVON RED

Red Devon river, fast and high,
When rain has deluged from the sky,
Carrying debris from fields and lanes,
Swept by the unforgiving rains.

For rainwater runoff brings red Devon soil
Rushing downhill to where the waters
   boil,
They bubble and swirl as if on fire,
As the water level grows still higher.

In hours few it will subside -
Red waters flown to join the tide,
And on the coast, some miles ahead,
The sea will drink in Devon red.

MERCURIAL RIVER

Mercurial river,

Yesterday, you boiled with rage,
in fierce, fiery temper,
your waters charging their angry way
downstream.

Today, calm and still,
you are as tranquil as a millpond,
with scarce a ripple to break
your smooth, flat surface.

Mercurial river,
what will you be tomorrow?

MOUNTAIN STREAM

The gently burbling stream
hurls itself furiously downhill,
as if with suicidal intent,
after twenty-four hours of mountain
   rain.

Swollen to ten times her usual size,
straining the bounds of common decency,
she thunders and roars her murderous
   way.

Like a bobsleigh team chasing an Olympic
   medal,
the surging force charges ever onward,
each drop that fell,
hellbent on reaching the ocean first.

DOWNDERRY BEACH

Layers of rock, laid bare at low tide,
moulded from malleable clay;
multi-coloured sculptures,
evolved over millennia.

Marbled pebbles, grey or pink-veined,
eye-catchingly beautiful,
worn smooth in the tumbling of time.

SHINGLE SHORE

The gentle metronomic swish
Of water, retreating from a shingle shore:
Each wave whooshes in, full of
    importance,
Then reverses slowly out,
As if embarrassed to have disturbed the
    peace.

They cannot creep in quietly, as on a
    sandy shore,
Just as children cannot run and play,
Except with squeals of pain.

TIDE ON SANDY SHORE

Virgin beauty restored:
Cleansed twice-daily,
Endlessly,
Tirelessly,
The invisible hand of the creator, re-
  creates.

Her newly-perfect complexion awaits
The first footprints,
The first sandcastles,
The inevitable spoiling of her perfection,
Endlessly,
Relentlessly,
As if in continuous jealous vendetta.

But like a blackboard eraser in
  classrooms of old,
The clockwork sea refreshes her ravaged
  beauty,
Wipes the slate clean,
Endlessly,
Uncomplainingly.

No matter the damage,
The saviour sea guards her honour,
And twice-daily,
Without fail,
Restores yet again her virgin beauty.

THE MOON

DAYTIME MOON

Moon hangs silently
in the afternoon sky,
a chalky thumbprint
on pale blue paper.

Outclassed by sister sun,
she waits patiently,
eager for evening,
and her own time to shine.

MOON-GAZING

The moon is a segment of white
   chocolate orange,
Suspended mid-air by an invisible
   thread,
Against a backdrop of jet-black velvet.

Mesmerised by her heavenly beauty,
I stand transfixed,
In the cooling midnight air.

LUNAR-CY

Waxing, waning,
Super new harvest,
Full blue honey-
Moon.

Made of green cheese,
The cow jumped over
The man in the
Paschal
Moon.

Blood black gibbous,
Strawberry crescent,
Purple eclipse of the
Moon.

THE JOY OF WALKING

COAST PATH IN THE MISTY DRIZZLE

Between birdsong and the gentle waves,
Nothing but my squelching footsteps
Plodding the empty coast path,
A solitary robin, my only friend.

Miles of sticky mud stretch out before
    me,
Though hidden by a teasing mist,
The raw, damp cold engulfs me,
As I make my way, stoically, along.

Please God the timetabled bus will arrive
At its scheduled destination, some hours
    hence,
But for now, head down, I trudge slowly
    onwards,
Towards our hopeful rendezvous.

CLOVELLY, WESTWARDS

Out on the path*, at the edge of land,
Infinity of blue beyond my right hand,
Welcome shade of woodland where
   bluebells abound,
A symphony of birdsong the only sound.

Steep rugged pathway zig-zags down and
   back up -
Just follow the acorn and trust to your
   luck!
Yellow clifftop gorse flowers buzzing
   with bees,
In the warmth of the sunshine and gentle
   spring breeze.

Whilst way down below, silent waves
   kiss the shore,
In perpetual motion, o'er and o'er,
Stresses and worries are left far behind,
A deep calm descends - I'm at peace with
   mankind.

*The South West Coast Path

COUNTRYSIDE CODE

On moorland or coast path,
Or down country lane,
Whate'er you take with you,
Please take home again;
Put litter in pocket,
Used cans in your pack,
Leave nothing but footprints
Along every track.

If your four-legged friends
Want to join in your stroll,
Keep them all close beside you,
Well under control,
Don't let them chase livestock,
Or else, with a gun,
A right angry farmer
May end all their fun!

To keep animals safe
And not let them stray,
Close each gate you open
As you go on your way;
Do not light fires -
Barbecues are a "no",
For long after you've left them,
Their embers still glow.

Take nothing but photos
On camera or phone,
Then enjoy them all later,
When safely back home,
For the countryside's beautiful,
Precious and rare,
Please treat it with reverence,
Respect and due care.

DOG WALK (a haiku)

Time to walk the dog;
Little legs need exercise,
Come rain, snow or fog.

FOOTPATHS

The narrow footpath heads enticingly
   uphill;
Curving out of sight,
It beckons me to follow...

A flock of sheep beyond a prickly hedge
Munch away the hours in quiet
   rumination,
Snatches of far-reaching views are
   glimpsed,
Tantalisingly, between tall trees.

Around each corner, new vistas unfold:
Changed perspectives, wider panoramas -
Endless possibilities enchant and delight
   me.

More paths turn off, encouraging
   exploration:
What lies this way?
Where does that one lead?
Hours to be spent in happy
   contemplation
Of the multitude of footpaths awaiting
   my feet.

MORNING CONSTITUTIONAL

The hasty wind rustles the serried ranks
   of larches
In the creosote-scented morning,
Golden leaves flutter gently to my feet,
Rooks converse noisily above my head,
And a grey squirrel skuttles up a handy
   bough.

The squelch beneath my boots betrays
   the recent rainfall,
As I inhale a cocktail of dankness and
   woodsmoke,
An early mist unwraps a sunny promise,
There is no silence! Yet a perfect peace,
As I turn for home, and the warm
   thought of breakfast.

PAS de DEUX

My heart and my head dance,
Hand-in-hand,
Along the open clifftop of the
South West Coast Path.

The scorching sun,
In an azure sky,
Plays delightedly with a crystal sea,
Bouncing sunbeams upon her,
Creating a myriad of diamonds
At every turn.

Here is peace.
Here is joy.
Here is utter contentedness.

My body, in the
Mundane monotony of my office,
Fails to gain control of the
Wilfully disobedient pair,
Who remain dancing,
Hand-in-hand,
Upon the open clifftop path.

THE EARLY WALKER

If the early bird catches the worm,
What of the early walker?

He catches the clarity of morning light,
The air resounding with sweetest
　　birdsong,
As he wanders the shady summer lanes,
As yet unpierced by scorching sun.

He breathes blue-blooded morning air,
Fresh and clean, unsullied;
He walks in dew-drenched morning
　　meadows,
And crunches virgin frost and snow.

He welcomes peace and solitude,
Claiming the countryside for his own,
Singularly possessing the space and
　　views,
While others still are slumbering.

He catches daytime unawares,
Unprepared for visitors,
In the innocence of her undress,
He espies nature's virgin beauty.

WINTER WALK

Mist shrouding the valley,
With blue sky above,
Observed from the clifftop,
On the coast path I love.

The winter sun cheers me,
Heart, soul and mind,
Its bright rays are balm
For ills of all kind.

PARTICULAR PLACES

GREENGATE

Walking down Greengate
as a lone cyclist struggles up,
standing on the pedals
to take the sharp right-handed corner.

Ahead, across the valley,
steep-sided mountains loom,
their bracken-covered flanks
lit by early morning rays.

No noise interrupts
the melodious birdsong,
and the persistent murmur
of nectar-seeking bees.

As the road levels out
alongside the brook,
gentle babbling
now accompanies the birdsong,
enriching the sweet sounds
of a lazy summer's day.

TROUTBECK

Small Lakeland village, ignored by passing
time,
Houses dating back to the sixteenth
century
Rise out of the fields, made of local
stone.

Historically, a handful of hamlets,
Built along a stagecoach route, north to
south,
Following the spring-line, with wells a-
plenty.

Farms cling to fellsides on the flanks of
Wansfell,
Undulating fields with no purpose but for
grazing
Adjoin the village street, as in ages long
ago.

Old stone barns, still agricultural,
Pepper the village, amidst all the
cottages,
Withstanding the trend for modern
conversions.

Little squat church, down in the valley,
With the Trout Beck babbling by,
Final resting place for the fortunate few.

An oasis of quiet,
As traffic screams up Kirkstone,
A timeless piece of paradise,
As life goes spinning by.

<u>TARN HOWS</u> (a haiku)

Soporific shore:
Gentle breeze on sunlit lake,
Who could ask for more?

DOWN BY THE FORD

The old road is broken, down by the ford,
Very few vehicles traverse it now,
And those that do, fear for their
    suspension!
A camel's hump of gravel rises up,
Legacy of tyres climbing out of the
    crossing,
And alluvial deposits, each time the brook
    floods.

Once maintained, now sadly neglected,
As insurance against the morning rat-
    run,
Pot-holed, deep-ditched, steeped in mud,
An obstacle course for determined drivers
Still brave enough to risk it,
Lurching and bouncing their way along.

Tall trees enclose the road by the ford,
Creating a magical, green-lit aura,
Shaded and cool in any weather;
The brook curls around the camel's hump,
To make a stony beach where children
    come to play,
As it meanders slowly through a right-
    angled bend.

Riders and walkers frequent the broken
    road,
Enjoying welcome shade from searing
    summer sun,
Cooling hot hooves as they wade through
    the ford,
Or keeping dry, by way of narrow bridge,
Their slow, measured progress
    uninterrupted,
As in centuries long gone by.

The old road is broken, down by the ford,
Now little used by anything vehicular,
Unless with four-wheel drive
Or beguiled by teasing sat nav,
Just a calm oasis for wildlife and walkers,
Beneath a green canopy, down by the
    ford.

HAMBEER LANE

Like a secret passage to a forgotten
    world,
Leafy green tunnel leads up from parched
    pavements
To a ridgetop path.

High Devon banks topped with ancient
    trees and hedgerows,
Slender branches touching, forming an
    oasis,
Welcome in heatwaves.

Mud-covered track betrays a broken
    metalled surface,
Testament to history – a link between
    villages,
Superseded now.

Along the ridgeway, unchanged for
    centuries,
Glimpses of the city appear periodically,
Across sun-scorched fields.

The dull throb of traffic makes a
     constant soundtrack
To the quiet timeless crunch of hoof, foot
     and paw,
On this sunken lane.

Old triangulation point, notes the
     observant,
Marking the summit of this once rural
     hill,
Past ever-present.

The sweet smell of hay wafts on warm
     summer breezes,
Insects buzz lazily and ponies whicker,
In an ancient world.

LOOE VALLEY LINE

A steep corkscrew descent at the head of
   the valley
Leads away from mainline, modern-day
   living,
Down into an ancient, ethereal world.

Here is history for the discerning:
The remnants of the union canal,
A reminder of a bygone age,
The seeds from which this branch line
   grew.

Now, mossy green trunks, twisted and
   gnarled,
Pass by the windows of the shuttling
   train,
A stream, idling its way down the valley,
Nourishes their ancient roots.

A statuesque heron awaits his chance
At one of many pools,
As the narrow, wooded valley starts to
   open out,
More waters rush to join, as if in
   conference,
As we head towards the sea.

Emerging from the tranquil, time-
   captured valley,
Waters widen into estuary,
Woodland gone, rushes appear on small
   islands,
Vast stretches of water in between,
And we know we're almost there.

Noisy seagulls have replaced the
   woodland birds,
As the train eases to a gentle halt
Beneath a wide, open sky,
Journey's end -
The sea!

CONSTITUTIONAL HILL

I wonder how many pairs of feet
Have trod this way before,
Unnumbered generations,
In countless days of yore,
Who trudged along the ridgeway,
To get from A to B,
Or wandered with a lover,
Perhaps more leisurely.

The dog-walkers whose daily route
Climbed up this very hill,
And lucky ones, who, just like me,
Are climbing on it still,
A route laid down in Saxon times,
So maps and records show,
Now a peaceful bridle path,
Where ancient trees still grow.

A rural scene that's little changed
Spreads out before my eye,
Of rolling hills and verdant trees,
And clear blue, open sky,
The same view that was gazed upon
By untold eyes before,
The eyes of those who walked this way,
In countless days of yore.

CABLE-CAR RIDE

Carried upwards - the only way to go
When the valley scorches at 33 degrees;
Orange capsules, soaring silently to giddy
   heights,
Disgorge their contents 600 metres
   higher.

A calm panorama - not cool or quiet!
Birdsong, grasshoppers and a cacophony
   of cow-bells
All clamour to be heard;
Like a Junior School percussion band
   ignoring their conductor,
The bells jangle on, each bar different,
Yet persistently monotonous.

The music fades as we amble slowly on,
Then, naughtily wilful, crescendos again!
Led by machine and urged on by man,
The cows move past us to pastures new.

A gradual decrescendo, then peace
   returns,
The insects and birds duet once more,
In the searing August heat
On Alpine peaks.

LE FRAYSSE HAUT

In the cool, clear calm
of a perfect summer morning,
where chickens wander freely
under verdant green trees,
hummingbird hawkmoths
dance on lilac lavender,
and nature drowses
beneath a cloudless blue sky.

Lizards scuttle crazily
and dive under paving,
bats roost behind shutters,
eager for evening,
fruit trees are heavy
with the promise of autumn,
God is in his heaven,
all is right with this world.

OBERTSDORF

Lazing on the balcony of my second-floor
    bedroom,
My feet gently warmed by the Alpine sun
Peeking cheekily beneath the wide Alpine
    eaves,
As if to say, "You can't hide from me!"

The church clock, hard by,
Marks the quarter hours of my indolence,
As I drift between conscious
And subconscious thought.

I am lulled by the chirruping of
    innumerable birds,
A distant goat-bleat, the bell of a cow,
The gentle rural fragrance wafting by
On the soporific summer breeze.

Content and lazy, I soon fall victim
To the deadly sin of sloth,
My body sighs,
My whole being relaxes.

Obertsdorf?
Nein! Der Himmel auf Erden!

A COUNTRY CALENDAR

JANUARY CHILL

Cold, damp winter air invades my lungs,
It squeezes my head and creeps into my
     bones,
As I wearily trudge up the hill.

A uniform panorama, in shades of grey,
Spreads out all around me,
As endless as January seems to be.

Bare-leafed branches, still as statues,
Stand out against a silver sky;
Spring, and warmth, have never seemed
     so far away!

LAKELAND WALK IN FEBRUARY

Mossy green walls that once were slate
  grey,
Defining the lane past the old stone barn,
Delicate snowdrops hide beneath hedges,
As if afraid of the strengthening sun.

Old badgers' sett with myriad entries,
Either side of a sheep-netted fence,
Network of footpaths, ripe for exploring,
With stimuli teasing every sense.

Wispy white clouds tickle the fell-tops,
Lichen-clad trees stand bare and stock
  still,
Daffodil buds promise explosion -
Carpet of yellow to cover the hills.

Clear panorama through bare brown
  branches,
Winter's raw beauty, rugged and cold,
The worst of the weather may still come
  upon us,
But with snowdrops and daffodils, spring
  is foretold.

MARCH EVENING

In the gathering gloom, as darkness
  beckons,
And a match is put to the fire,
Starlings murmur their intention to
  roost,
Owl stretches and checks her attire.

The colours of day fade to dull
  monochrome,
Bright flowers now appear shades of grey,
Badgers are roused from their daytime
  sleep,
As birds bid "Goodnight" to the day.

The mercury dips - is Jack Frost abroad?
Come morning, will green become white?
The lambs' tails festooning the hazel
  twigs shiver,
As dusk slips headlong into night.

APRIL, FOOL

April, master of fools,
Entices people out of doors
By dint of golden sunshine,
Then empties clouds
Upon their unsuspecting heads!

MAYPOLE DANCING

Standing stock still,
Ears strained for the opening chords,
A mix of worry and concentration
Writ large upon young faces –
Will we go the right way?
Will the ribbons tangle?
What if I can't remember?!

The music starts;
Bowing to partners,
Young feet start to skip around the
    maypole,
Ribbons clasped tightly,
Frowns of concentration,
Mouths counting,
Bodies weaving in and out,
Past their friends,
In ever decreasing circles.
Slowly, bright patterns emerge
Around and about the tall wooden pole,
A different design for each different
    dance,
Increasingly complex as the display wears
    on;
Faces relax, smiles replace frowns,
As each dance is achieved without error.

At last, an intricate weave decorates the
    pole –
The final triumph of double plait –
We've done it!
The music ends with one last chord,
They bow again, in triumph now,
Ecstatic smiles wreathing their faces,
Then, duty done, it's off for ice-cream -
May Day is over for another year!

UNPREDICTABLE JUNE

Flaming June, the height of summer:
Long sunny days under cloudless blue
  skies,
Suntanned bodies relaxing by pools,
Hay-making,
Village fêtes,
Lazy days on hazy beaches,
Water endlessly kissing the shore,
Children playing noisily through long light
  evenings,
Bathed in the glorious warmth of
  summer.

Chilly June, though height of summer:
Cloudy skies threatening rain,
Anxious faces scanning forecasts,
Cancelled sports days,
Indoor picnics,
Fish and chips on breezy beaches,
Huddled in fleeces, trying to keep warm,
Brides in brightly coloured wellies
Splashing through puddles to reach the
  church door.

Unpredictable June!

THE TROUTBECK VALLEY IN JULY

The sky is as clear as in my rose-tinted
   memories,
Endless, unbroken blue, stretched out like
   virgin canvas,
Awaiting the first brush-strokes of the
   master's hand.

The sun, burning bright, creeps lazily
   through the heavens,
Arcing up over Sallows to drop down
   behind Wansfell,
Taking no prisoners with her scorching
   rays.

No sounds to disturb me except those of
   Mother Nature:
A percussive wind plays through full-
   leafed trees,
Adding accompaniment to song of birds
   and bees.

No traffic whines up Kirkstone, no quad-
   bikes cross the fields,
The soporific sun casts a spell upon the
   valley,
As it peacefully slumbers in the heat of
   midday.

AUGUST HEDGEROWS

Late summer hedges encroach upon the
    roadway,
As if to arrest the flow of passing cars,
Bright sun, peeping through leafy tunnels,
Creeps around the outstretched fronds.

Laden with a wealth of fruits,
Branches bow down with weight of their
    largesse:
The first blackberries are ripening for
    harvest
As acorns and beechnuts start to fall to
    the ground.

Holidaymakers still flock to the beaches,
Cursing the unaccustomed narrowness of
    lanes,
Scantly aware of the opulence of nature,
Just encroaching summer hedges,
    impeding their way.

SEPTEMBER DAY

Crisp, clear morning
Breathes fresh promise of a bright new
    day;
Early chill
Submits to fiery noonday heat;
Perfect summer afternoon,
Ere the sun slips laughingly away;
Night shivers in,
Autumn approaches.

GOLDEN OCTOBER

Golden brown, the falling leaves
Flutter gently in the autumn breeze,
While deep red acers, neat and small,
Give colour-burst o'er garden wall.

Fellside ghylls rush, all a-quiver,
Eager to meet the valley's river,
Like silver streaks, they tumble down
The bracken-covered hills so brown.

Old barn doors, propped open wide,
Give glimpse of hay bales stacked inside,
Treasured up, behind the door,
For whatever winter has in store.

Hazy sunshine still has power
To set the wind-blown lake on fire,
The ripples dance, just like the leaves,
In the strengthening autumn breeze.

BONFIRE NIGHT

With words of Milton's poem* buzzing
   round in their heads,
Excited children pour out of school,
Eager for fun, on the fifth of November.

"Remember, remember," they chant as
   they run,
In anticipation of forthcoming darkness,
And spectacular scenes they hope it will
   bring.

Passing the pyre on the village green,
Minds race with memories from a year
   before,
Of leaping flames and bejewelled skies.

As darkness falls, clad in warm scarves
   and jackets,
Excitedly, they gather round the waiting
   bonfire,
In age-old tradition, as their parents
   before.

Scarce able to wait, the tension thickens,
Until finally, countdown begins:
"3, 2, 1..." Whoosh!

Sudden flames leap through the pile of
   pallets,
Old furniture and garden rubbish,
Well-doused from handy cans of petrol.

Delighted faces glow warm orange,
Transfigured by reflected firelight,
As they wait for the fireworks to begin.

The air explodes as sudden gunshot,
The sky ignites in glorious colours,
Sparkling like expensive, well-cut jewels.

"Oohs" and "ahhs" echo round the bonfire,
Faces turned heavenwards in pure
   delight,
Each explosion eliciting fresh gasps of
   joy.

All too soon, a sky-splitting crescendo
Announces the display has reached its
   finale...
Then night returns as the air falls silent.

Ears ringing, adults watch the dying
   embers,
Eating and drinking as peace is restored,
Before small children are rounded up for
   home.

Tomorrow, they will all relive it eagerly
   in classrooms,
Creating coloured artwork and combining
   clever words,
Recreating the remembrance of the
   treasonous plot.

"Remember, remember, the fifth of
   November," *
They'll chant as they work.
And they will!

* from the English translation of John
Milton's (1626) poem, 'In Quintum Novembris'

FROSTY DECEMBER *(a haiku)*

   Cold, crunchy morning;
   The grass starts to glisten as
   Daylight is dawning.

THROUGH THE SEASONS

METEOROLOGICAL SPRING

The first day of March -
Meteorologically, spring has sprung,
Sky clears in celebration,
Clouds stop their weeping,
Momentarily, at least.

Short days now are lengthening,
Sun is slowly strengthening,
Life returns gradually to hedgerow and
    branch,
As the iron grip of chilly winter
Relaxes into sun-kissed spring.

VERNAL EQUINOX

A perfect parity of day and night,
Equal opportunity for darkness and light,
Neither one dominant,
Neither subservient,
But a harmony of equality,
As the sun crosses the celestial equator,
And Earth moves away from the darkness
   of winter,
Towards the long, light days of summer.

Held together in a brief moment of
   equivalence,
Of balance, they mirror one another,
Before darkness starts to lose his power
And daylight slowly regains hers,
For just one day, twice a year,
They are equal partners,
A perfect parity
Of daytime and night.

SPRING

Jewels of dew
Bedeck the lawn with diamonds,
Birds serenade their lovers
Beneath a virgin blue sky,
The leaden oppressiveness of winter
Thaws, under the gaze
Of the strengthening sun.

Nature's early colour-show erupts -
Delicate crocuses nod politely,
Carpets of daffodils wave
    enthusiastically,
Dancing excitedly in the lengthening
    days.

Hearts rejoice,
Smiles return,
Spring is come!

LATE SPRING

Flashes of bluebells in bright spring-green
    hedges,
Tiny new leaflets bursting from bud,
White hawthorn flowers and blossom on
    fruit trees,
Lanes slowly drying from quagmires of
    mud.

Primroses, cowslips, crocus and
    celandine,
Splashes of yellow of every hue,
Gentle strolls in the lengthening
    evenings,
Lightening mornings still damp with the
    dew.

Around every corner the world is
    awaking,
The bleakness of winter now slipping
    away,
Early spring promises now being
    honoured,
As brighter and warmer becomes each
    new day.

AWOL: SPRING

Winter leapt straight into summer that
   year,
With scarcely a nod towards spring.
Lanes, for months ankle-deep in mud,
Were dust-baths a mere fortnight later,
Overflowing water-butts soon ran dry,
As gardeners struggled
To hydrate their parched plots.

Winter leapt straight into summer that
   year,
With little time to acclimatise.
Booted, fleece-clad figures,
Swaddled for endless, cold, wet months,
Morphed overnight into beach babes,
Bare burnt limbs testament
To total unpreparedness.

Winter leapt straight into summer that
   year.
Washing, long-confined to mechanical
   dryers,
Danced excitedly on sun-drenched lines;
Garden furniture, liberated from storage,
Pressed into immediate use,
The tempting scent of barbecues
Drifting on balmy evening breezes.

Winter leapt straight into summer that
   year,
Although spring flowers had appeared in
   abundance.
Nature, confused, sent mixed messages:
Weather remained resolutely in the past,
Whilst flora and fauna strained excitedly
   forward,
Impatient for seasonal change,
The year winter leapt straight into
   summer.

HAY MEADOWS

Buttercups dance with flowering grasses,
In the hay meadow, down by the brook,
Standing tall in the nourishing sun,
Absorbing her rays, storing her energy,
Locking it in for cold winter days.

Slain, they lie in the summer meadow,
Side by side in the dehydrating sun,
Then, light as air, they are gathered
   together,
Baled up, ready for forthcoming winter -
Precious food for barren days.

SUMMER BOUNTY

Golden fields, close-cropped for winter,
Precious largesse safely gathered in,
Hedgerows bursting with ripe juicy
    berries,
Nature's bounty for pie, jam or gin.

Fat juicy pears, ripening apples,
Plump red tomatoes, swelling courgettes,
Cabbages, carrots, beans and potatoes,
Produce-show winners of coloured
    rosettes.

Barns are full up now, cupboards
    replenished,
Long sunny days supply food for us all,
Harvest is gathered, ready for winter,
Nature providing for great and for small.

SUMMER INTO AUTUMN

When morning chill greets the early
  walker,
And dewy diamonds sparkle on the grass,
When juicy blackberries beguile him from
  the hedgerows,
He knows that autumn is approaching,
  fast.

When twittering swallows meet upon the
  phone wires,
Gathering for their migratory flight,
When harvest is gathered and straw bales
  are binded,
He knows that autumn is almost in sight.

When verdant trees change their rich
  summer clothing,
Their once-green leaves become golden
  and red,
When children play conkers and start to
  build bonfires,
He knows summer has slipped into
  autumn instead.

AUTUMN MORNING

Crepuscular rays burst through the still-
   green canopy,
Lighting up the dewdrops heavy on the
   grass,
Vapour rises slowly from trees in the
   meadow,
Like steam from a hidden row of old
   locomotives,
As the rising sun warms the early
   autumn morning.

Rowan trees and brambles bend low
   overhead,
Offering a richness of colourful berries,
Swallows are circling above the meadow,
Preparing themselves for their overseas
   flights,
In the quiet gentleness of the early
   autumn morning.

Their warm breath visible in the chilly
   autumn air,
Cows munch peacefully across the sunny
   meadow,
Enjoying autumn grazing ahead of winter
   hay;
Walkers grab jackets before heading out
In the growing chill of the early autumn
   morning.

SHINY BROWN CONKERS

Shiny brown conkers, split from their
    cases,
Yellow-green acorns, spilt to the ground,
Hazel-nut shells and black splats of
    berries,
Nature's litter, strewn all around.

Sweet chestnut shells along the footpath,
Like a prickle of hedgehogs out for a
    stroll,
Richness of fruits half-hidden in
    hedgerows,
Nature's bounty gives food for us all.

Dank, misty mornings with dewdrops a-
    glistening,
Chill in the air as the night lingers on,
Curled yellow leaves that crunch under
    footsteps,
Nature's message - summer has gone.

Bonfire smoke as the afternoons darken,
Scents of autumn now filling the air,
Mushrooms sprout and berries turn
    scarlet,
So nature tells us, autumn is here.

OFF-SEASON

The welcome silence of solitude,
Broken only by birdsong,
Intermittent bleating and the
Babbling of tumbling becks.

Half-empty roads - no traffic jams!
A warm seat by the fireside
In village pub or tea-shop,
Hard-earned by winter walking.

Miles of empty muddy footpaths,
Hills bedecked in mist or rain-cloud,
Careful plans for hiking
Before the short day closes in.

Two owls in conversation,
Their calls filling the darkness,
Echoing through the valley
In the cool, crisp winter air.

WINTER TREES

Against a greying winter sky,
Delicate branches stand,
As if on infinite canvas,
Painted by God's own hand.

85

MONOCHROME WINTER

White window frames
In grey cottage walls,
White water tumbling
O'er grey stony falls,
Grey Herdwick sheep,
Grazing up on the fells,
Old grey stone troughs
By the spring-water wells.

Grey dry-stone walls
Beneath dark leaden sky,
Smoky-grey clouds,
Threatening to cry,
White snowdrop flowers
By black tarmac road,
Bordered by walls that are
Crumbling and bowed.

Black silhouettes
Of trees 'gainst the grey
Of the monochrome sky,
This bleak winter day,
Grey plume of smoke
From old cottage fire,
Ascends to the heavens,
Higher and higher.

Grey chips of slate
On the paths up the hills,
Do naught to dispel
Those grey winter chills,
Like a black and white photo
From camera of old,
The bleak wintry landscape
Is barren and cold.

The whole panorama
A monochrome scene,
Of black, white and grey,
Save touches of green,
For moss on the stones
And grass in the fields,
The singular colour
This wintry scene yields.

THE WEATHER

LOW CLOUD IN THE VALLEY

The sun is shining,
Somewhere above the low clouds that
   cover the hilltops,
Brighter patches of white betray her
   attempts to break through,
But the clouds hunker down, fiercely
   possessive,
Like a dog guarding a particularly juicy
   bone.

The unmistakable skylines have
   disappeared,
No sight of the cairns that proudly mark
   the summits,
Usually visible from the valley bottom;
The hills on both sides are shrouded in a
   grey-white cloak.

The valley shrinks further as the clouds
   roll down,
Lower slopes now gathered under the
   misty blanket;
With recognisable landmarks hidden from
   view,
The valley loses its particular identity.

Eventually, the sun will win the battle
    for supremacy,
Clouds banished, the landscape will
    regain its personality,
But all the while it's hidden by a cloak of
    invisibility,
It could be almost any valley, anywhere!

MIST ON THE LAKE

Enveloped in a melancholy mist,
Lake waters fade into oblivion,
Just a gentle lapping on the shore,
At the edge of invisibility.

FORECAST RAIN *(a haiku)*

Dog-walking early,
Trying to beat the downpours.
Timed it wrong. Bugger!

RAIN

Rain,
Turns roads into rivers,
Meadows to meres.

Rain,
Wreaks havoc with railways,
Cancelling trains.

Rain,
Floods towns and villages,
Businesses and homes.

Rain,
Disrupts fêtes and picnics,
Bane of blushing brides.

Rain,
Cleanses dirt from pavements,
Washes grime away.

Rain,
Replenishes reservoirs,
Rivers, lakes and streams.

Rain,
Refreshes parched pasture,
Enables crops to grow.

Rain,
Nourisher of nature,
Life-blood of us all.

Rain -
Irritating,
Plan-changing,
Totally maddening,
Wonderfully refreshing and
Life-giving,
RAIN!

IMPENDING STORM

Lightning crackles across the sky,
Thunder rolls over the hills,
An ominous oppression hangs overhead,
Heavy clouds poised to unleash their fury.

From the still, charged air, winds whip
   up,
Dried debris swirling under leaden sky,
A sense of foreboding fills the waiting air,
As the first fat drops splatter down.

CLOUDBURST

Washed by a sudden biblical downpour,
The usually muddy footpath is clean,
Broken tarmac and cobbles newly
   revealed.

Clouds emptying themselves upon the
   hilltop,
A brown torrent chose the way of least
   resistance,
A rushing river poured downhill, sweeping
   all before it,
Seeking out the nearest drain in which to
   disappear,
Dumping, in any available place,
Its load of leaves
And mud
And grit.

Cloudburst over, only a trail of debris
   remained,
Evidencing the recent deluge:
Small clumps of abandoned leaves
Dotted along the clean path's edge,
Like markers on a cross-country course,
Pointing out the way;

A sea of mud,
Trapped in the natural dip of the lane,
Outside a country pub;
Grit and leaves
Spreadeagled across the road,
Signposting the torrent's pathway,
The escape-route used just hours before.

Over coming days, normality returns,
Winds and traffic clear the leaf-strewn
    roads,
(Although the mud by the pub remains ad
    infinitum),
Falling leaves and berries once again
Strew the recently clear path,
Mud and litter accumulate once more,
All along the hilltop...

Until the next time the heavens are torn
    asunder,
And footpaths perchance become stream-
    beds again.

AFTER THE STORM *(a haiku)*

Deluge aftermath:
Footpaths morphed to quagmires,
Dog requiring bath!

LAKE DISTRICT RAINOMETER

Low cloud,
Misty dampness,
Mizzle,
Drizzle,
Light refreshing rain.

Intermittent showers,
Persistent rainfall,
Steadily heavy downpour.

Stair-rods,
Hail,
Torrential deluge,
Crashing thunderstorm.

Lakeland life continues,
Whatever the state of rain!

NOCTURNAL NIGHTMARE

Trying to sleep
Drip
Drip-drip
While the raindrops fall
Drip-drip
Drip
From the trees that hang over
Drip-drip
Drip-drip-drip
My caravan roof.

Drip
Drip-drip
Drip
Drip-drip-drip
Drip-drip
Drip
Drip-drip.

No regular rhythm
Drip-drip
Drip
To lull me to sleep
Drip-drip-drip
Drip-drip

Just sudden bursts
Drip-drip-drip-drip
Drip-drip
Drip
Drip-drip
Each time my eyelids close.

Drip
Drip-drip-drip
Drip-drip
Drip
Drip-drip
Drip-drip-drip
Drip-drip.

A sudden explosion
DRIP-DRIP-DRIP-DRIP-DRIP
DRIP-DRIP-DRIP
DRIP-DRIP
DRIP
Like beating hammers
DRIP-DRIP
DRIP-DRIP-DRIP-DRIP
DRIP-DRIP-DRIP
DRIP-DRIP
The wind batters the branches
DRIP-DRIP
DRIP-DRIP-DRIP

DRIP

DRIP-DRIP

Over again.

Drip

Drip-drip

Drip

Drip-drip-drip

Drip

Drip-drip

Drip-drip-drip.

Drip-drip

Drip

Drip-drip-drip

Drip-drip

Drip

Drip-drip-drip

Drip-drip.

Drip

Drip-drip-drip

Drip-drip.

Drip-drip-drip

Drip

Drip-drip...

RAINY DAY *(a haiku)*

What if the sky cries?
We'll splash through mud and puddles,
Until it all dries.

SUNSHINE AFTER RAIN

A sunny morning after weeks of rainfall
Is as chocolate following the Lenten fast:
Senses heighten, pulses race,
Leaden hearts are light again,
The world comes back into focus,
Colours deepen and intensify,
Sweet floral fragrances fill the clear air,
As birds sing out their unadulterated joy.

HEATWAVE

Early August, and the
first few yellow leaves
flutter gently to the ground,
legacy of recent heatwave.

Dry brown verges,
dying grass and drooping shrubs,
evidence endless days
beneath a scorching summer sun.

Farmers rub their hands in glee,
one eye on the forecast,
anticipating harvest
will be quickly gathered in.

Holiday-makers retire nightly
to their hotels and caravans,
seeking cooling showers
and reaching for the after-sun.

Long hot days of endless sunshine,
yet autumn waits around the corner,
foreshown by first few yellow leaves,
fluttering gently to the ground.

DROUGHT

Dry and parched, the barren earth lies
    gasping,
Scorched yellow fields where once, green
    grass grew,
Day follows day, testing the mercury,
Memories of heatwaves come into sharp
    view.

Mountainside becks are all eerily silent,
Gulleys and ditches not muddy, but dry,
Far distant thunder makes farmers'
    hearts quicken,
Day after day while the mercury's high.

Drowned farmsteads surface from
    reservoir graveyards,
Valleys once filled with the living, now
    dead,
Withered leaves fall, impatient for
    autumn,
Turning dry streambeds orange and red.

Worry-lined faces scan every forecast,
Predictions continue - more of the same,
Despite our intelligence and our
    inventions,
We can do nothing but pray for the rain.

FROSTY MORNING

The frost lies thick upon the grass,
The air is cold and chill,
The lazy sun is creeping up,
Beyond the grey-green hill.

The leafy carpet sparkles
In her early morning rays,
And crunches 'neath the walker's feet,
These glorious winter days.

CHANGE IN THE WEATHER

No fresh frost,
But yesterday's still lingers
On sheltered verges and down wooded
  lanes.

A beautiful red sunrise
Warns us of the next storm, rolling in –
The blue-skied days of winter
Are now past.

ROBIN ON A SNOWY MORNING

Robin perches atop the snowy wall,
Observing the frozen world about him,
Changed overnight into a winter
    wonderland,
As beautiful as any Christmas card or
    cake.

All around is an eerie silence,
The usual sounds of morning absent
    today,
For little traffic attempts to travel
Along the narrow and ungritted lanes.

Well-wrapped dog-walkers venture out,
Their charges bouncing excitedly
Through the freshly fallen snow,
Barking at the strange new world that
    greets them.

From the safety of his snow-capped wall,
Robin watches, silently,
His bright black eye missing nothing
In this cold, unfriendly world.

THE BEAST FROM THE EAST

Cosily relaxing in my glass bubble,
I'm entranced by the snowflakes dancing
    outside -
Now a slow waltz, now a crazy jive,
As if following an inaudible, ever-
    changing beat.

Frenzied, yet bizarrely calming,
Their soporific beauty mesmerises me,
Lost to all else but their stark, white
    beauty,
I cannot help but watch their
    monotonous falling.

Hypnotised, I gaze on, endlessly;
Engulfed by the silence of the frozen
    white world,
A strange warm peace descends.

WIND

The raging wind, in indignant ire,
Poured out his frustration in celestial
   temper,
Roaring angrily, like a lion,
Unleashing the full force of his fierce fury
On unsuspecting earth below.

Unaware of any transgressions,
Cattle continued their considered
   munching,
Stoically plodding their way across
   pasture,
Seemingly oblivious to the ranting wind,
For they have heard his anger oft before.

Walkers, huddled into well-zipped
   jackets,
Heads down, plodded on,
Dogs, holding tightly to their battered
   ears,
Trotted faithfully beside,
Day-dreaming of cosy firesides and bones.

Still, wind raged and bellowed,
Holding nothing back, venting his
 vexations,
Showing not one ounce of mercy
For battered Earth, languishing below,
Just a selfish desire to discharge his
 pent-up wrath.

Eventually, like an exhausted toddler,
 post-tantrum,
Wind was spent,
Rant over, nothing gained,
He crept ashamedly away,
Tail between his trembling legs.

And just the hint of a whispered "Sorry,"
Hung in the now quiet air.

www.ingramcontent.com/pod-product-compliance
Ingram Content Group UK Ltd.
Pitfield, Milton Keynes, MK11 3LW, UK
UKHW031022181224
452569UK00004B/353